What Happens When We Recycle

Paper?

Jillian Powell

W
FRANKLIN WATTS
LONDON • SYDNEY

This edition copyright © Franklin Watts 2014
338 Euston Road, London NW1 3BH

Franklin Watts Australia
Level 17/207 Kent Street
Sydney NSW 2000

Editor: Julia Bird
Designer: DR Ink
Art Director: Jonathan Hair

Picture credits: Agstockusa/SPL: 25b; Beanstalk/Waste Watch:
11; Vicki Coombs/Ecoscene: 16; Cutlura/Corbis; 12t; Patrick
Dumas/Eurelios/SPL: 15t; Elnur/Shutterstock: 8cl; Graham
Flack/Waste Watch: 14, 17b, 23, 24; David R. Frazier PL/Alamy:
7; David R. Frazier/SPL: 21t; Will Iredale/Shutterstock: 6; JG
Photography/Alamy: 18; Kmitu/Shutterstock: 8cr; R.
Maisonneuve/Publiphoto Diffusion/SPL: 22; Tatiana
Markow/Sygma/Corbis: 19; Moodboard/Corbis: 10, 15cl;
Susumu Nishinaga/SPL: 17cl; Kenneth V Pilon/Shutterstock: 20;
Mark Poprocki/Shutterstock: 25c; Diana Rich/Shutterstock: 8c.
Don Smith/Alamy: 9; Tom Stewart/Corbis: 12b; Peter
Turnley/Corbis: 21; Justin Kase zthreez/Alamy: 13.

A CIP catalogue record for this book
is available from the British Library

ISBN: 978 1 4451 3029 3

Dewey Classification: 363.72'88

Printed in China

Franklin Watts is a division of
Hachette Children's Books,
an Hachette UK company
www.hachette.co.uk

Contents

About paper

How it is made

Paper is a **material** made from plants, such as wood, rice, cotton, linen and sugar cane. These plants all contain **fibres** that stick together when mixed with water to make a **pulp**, which is dried as flat sheets to make paper. Today, most paper is made from wood.

A pine forest plantation. Wood from these trees is used to make paper.

Wood to paper

Before it can be made into paper, wood is chopped into little pieces or chips. These are taken to a **paper mill** where they are turned into paper.

Wood chips are used to make paper.

Different types

There are many different types of paper, from white writing paper and glossy magazine paper, to **corrugated** card used for packaging food and drinks.

How we use paper

● Paper products

We use paper in homes, schools and businesses. Paper can be made into books, newspapers, magazines, kitchen and toilet rolls, tissues, babies' nappies, envelopes and bank notes. Card, which is stiff, strong paper, can be used to make boxes and packaging.

> We use paper in lots of different ways every day.

JUST THE FACTS

Paper and card make up almost 20% of our rubbish. On average, each UK household throws away about 4 kilograms of paper and card every week.

Waste

People often waste paper. In the UK, we use around 12.5 million tonnes of paper and card every year. About 66% is **recycled** and the rest is burned or dumped in **landfill sites**.

GREEN GUIDE

There are many ways we can reduce paper waste. One is writing or printing on both sides of a piece of paper. It is also good to reuse paper, for example wrapping paper, whenever you can.

You can reuse paper by shredding or scrunching it up and using it to help make garden **compost**.

Why recycle paper?

New paper

Wasting paper means that more trees have to be cut down to make new paper. Paper mills also use a lot of **energy** to make paper, creating **carbon emissions** which are causing **climate change**.

Most paper now comes from **managed plantations** where trees are specially grown for paper.

The environment

Paper mills use less water and between 70 and 80% less energy recycling paper than making new paper. Saving energy cuts down carbon emissions. Recycling paper also cuts down on water **pollution**. This is because new paper is often **bleached** with chemicals.

Landfill problems

When paper goes into landfill, it rots down and creates **methane gas**. This is one of the gases causing climate change.

Landfill space in the UK is running out.

Collection

● Recycling boxes

Some paper and card is collected from households in recycling boxes or bins. The paper can be separated from other waste by householders before they put it out for collection. It can also be collected from mixed bins with plastics, cans and other recyclable materials.

Many people combine a shopping trip with a visit to the recycling bins.

Neighbourhoods can join in with paper recycling schemes.

GREEN GUIDE

Make sure that paper you put out for recycling is clean and dry.

Auto sort machines

Waste paper can also be taken to paper banks in supermarket car parks. Some supermarkets have 'auto sort' machines that can separate the different types of waste people put in them. They use cameras, **infra-red** light and air jets to sort and separate different materials. Some can sort up to 80 different products each minute.

Lorries

Recycling lorries collect paper and card from homes, paper banks and from some shops and offices. They take it by road to paper sorting centres.

Paper recycling lorries can hold several tonnes of waste paper.

Sorting

Mixed waste

Paper and card that are collected in mixed bins have to be separated from other waste. This is often done by hand. It can also be done by machine. The mixed waste passes along a fast **conveyor belt** and infra-red rays are shone onto it. The machines use air jets to separate out the different materials.

Infra-red light reflects differently off each material. A computer can then tell what the material is.

JUST THE FACTS

Paper was one of the first materials to be recycled. Today it makes up about 40% of waste collected for recycling.

Grading

Paper and card are sorted and **graded** ready for recycling. There are several grades of paper, from white paper to newspapers and magazines. Workers sort the paper and card as it moves along a conveyor belt. They flatten boxes and remove staples or paper clips and tape.

Workers wear thick gloves to protect their hands.

A forklift truck lifts the paper bales into a storage area.

Baling

The card and paper are sent along a conveyor belt into a machine that packs them into flat **bales**. The machine ties the bales with wire. The bales are ready to be taken to a paper mill for recycling.

GREEN GUIDE

You can help by removing any staples or tape before you send paper or card for recycling.

Pulping

Screening

At the paper mill, paper and card go into a screening machine. This separates newspapers and magazines from smaller, mixed paper. After this, the paper is put on to two conveyor belts.

The paper on the conveyor belts travels along at around six metres per second!

Cleaning

The paper and card then pass under infra-red lights. These pick out any leftover bits of plastic or metal. Air jets fire them away into waste chutes.

? DID YOU KNOW?

The fibres in paper are held together with **lignin** which acts like glue. Pulping breaks down the lignin, separating the fibres.

Water

The paper is now ready for pulping. The pulping machines add water, which separates the fibres in the paper to form a wet pulp. Paper mills use lots of water. They recycle the water as many times as possible before sending it to a water treatment plant for cleaning.

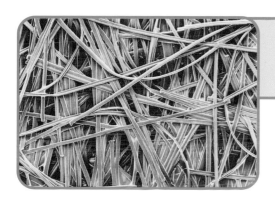

Paper fibres seen under a powerful **microscope**.

JUST THE FACTS

Paper can only be recycled about six times. This is because each time the fibres get shorter, until they start to break down.

Paper mills use water for pulping and washing the paper fibres.

Cleaning

The machine is spinning and mixing the paper pulp.

Spinning

The wet pulp passes through **sieves** that remove any non-paper materials like staples, paper clips or tape that were missed at the sorting centre. Big drums then spin the pulp. This rubs the paper fibres together and helps to loosen and separate out bits of glue and plastics.

De-inking

The pulp now has any ink removed. Ink is removed from the paper fibres by washing with soap and then rinsing with more water.

Flotation

The ink is removed by pumping the pulp into **flotation tanks** which act like giant washing machines. Soap and other chemicals are added, then air is blown through the pulp. The inky foam that collects on the surface is skimmed off.

DID YOU KNOW? ?

The sludge left over from paper making can be burned as fuel for the paper mills. It is also used in compost or to make bricks.

Large flotation tanks clean and wash the pulp.

Whitening

● Paper colour

Some recycled paper looks dull and greyish in colour because of ink and lignin in the pulp. In time, lignin and sunlight can react to turn paper yellow, which is why old newspapers go yellow. Paper mills use different methods to whiten and brighten paper.

Sunlight makes old newspapers yellow and brittle.

? DID YOU KNOW?

The brightness of paper is measured by the amount of light it reflects. White office paper reflects up to 90% light, but paper bags may only reflect 20 or 30% light.

White paper

To make white paper, the paper fibres are bleached. The pulp is soaked in bleaching chemicals, such as **chlorine**, then passes through a fine screen to remove any waste materials.

Bleaching is used to make paper as white as possible.

Better bleaching

Bleaching produces large amounts of polluted waste water which is bad for the **environment**. **Oxygen** can also be used to whiten paper fibres. This causes less pollution than bleaching with chemicals.

This river in China is polluted by bleached waste from a nearby paper mill.

GREEN GUIDE

Look out for recycled paper which has the label 'chlorine-free'.

Paper making

● Paper machines

The pulp is now ready to be made into recycled paper. First, it is pumped between giant wire screens to make a web of paper fibres. The web goes between felt presses that squeeze out water, then under vacuum rollers. Next, it passes over steam-heated rollers that boil off any remaining water.

As the pulp dries, samples of it are taken for testing.

22

Bonding

As water is removed from the paper, the fibres rub closer together until they join to form a single sheet. Most writing and printing paper is about 7 to 8 fibres thick. Some paper has **starch** added to make it smooth for printing and writing. Paper can also be coated with **china clay** to make it glossy.

Huge reels roll the paper up.

Reels

Rollers smooth and polish the paper, then feed it onto a giant reel. Each reel weighs about 45 tonnes and has to be carried by robot machines around the mill.

? DID YOU KNOW?

Paper fibres bond together without any glue when pulp is dried and pressed.

New products

recycled A5 notebook
100 perforat
Ruled

recycled
DL white envelopes
size 110mm x 220mm
50 pack

100%
Recycled
paper

These notepads and envelopes are made from 100% recycled paper.

Uses of recycled paper

Recycled paper is often used for printing newspapers or magazines. It can also be used to make a variety of recycled paper products, including paper pads and notebooks, toilet rolls, kitchen paper, tissues and greetings cards.

?

DID YOU KNOW?

In the UK today, newspapers and corrugated card packaging are made from 100% recycled paper fibres. Most tissues and wrapping paper also have a high content of recycled fibres.

Packaging

Recycled paper can be used to make packaging such as egg cartons, Jiffy bags and boxes.

GREEN GUIDE

Look out for the recycling symbol that shows the amount of recycled fibre a paper product contains.

Made From 100% Recycled Materials

Other products

Recycled paper fibres can also be used in making paints, loft **insulation** and road building.
Tea bag papers and card can be shredded for use as bedding for horses and other animals.

JUST THE FACTS

It can take just seven days from start to finish to recycle a newspaper.

Recycled paper fibres make soft bedding for cows and other farm animals.

What you can do

CASE STUDY

At Filton Hill Primary School in Bristol, pupils attended a workshop led by paper artist Bridget Ely. They then made their own recycled paper out of waste materials and used it to make Easter cards. They took the cards home in decorative folders made from recycled cereal packets.

5 top tips for paper recyclers:

1	2	3	4	5
Keep paper clean and dry for recycling.	Remove staples and tape and wash and squash cartons.	Shred or scrunch newspaper and add to compost bins.	Look out for recycled paper products.	Above all, try to reduce the amount of paper you are using.

Paper bead wrist-band

You will need:
Leftover or scrap paper
Glue
Scissors
Thin string

Step 1
Choose the colours you want for your beads: they could be football team colours or to match clothes.

Step 2
Cut strips of paper in each colour about one centimetre wide and ten centimetres long.

Step 3
Spread some glue over half of one strip, then roll up the paper, beginning with the glue-free short end. As you roll, leave a hole in the middle that the thread can go through.

Step 4
Keep going until you have enough paper beads to make the wrist-band.

Step 5
String the beads onto the string. Check the length on your wrist, then cut the string and tie into a neat knot.

Glossary

Bales Large bundles of material.

Bleached Whitened with chemicals.

Carbon emissions Gases containing carbon dioxide. Carbon emissions are believed to be causing climate change.

China clay A fine white clay.

Chlorine A gas used for cleaning and bleaching.

Climate change A gradual change in the climate of our planet.

Compost A mix of materials that break down to make soil richer.

Conveyor belt A belt that moves to carry things along.

Corrugated Ridged or folded.

Energy Heat or power.

Environment Surroundings.

Fibres Long threads.

Flotation tanks Tanks that hold water.

Graded Ranked by quality.

Infra-red A kind of light ray.

Insulation Layers of material that stop heat escaping.

Landfill sites Places where rubbish is buried under the ground.

Lignin A glue-like substance found in wood pulp.

Managed plantations Forests that have been specially planted for harvesting trees.

Material A substance that something else is made from.

Methane gas A colourless gas that can cause climate change.

Microscope An instrument used to look at very small objects. A microscope makes the object appear a lot bigger than it is.

Oxygen A gas found in air.

Paper mill A place where paper is made.

Papyrus A tall plant that grows near water.

Pollution Harmful substances that get into soil, water or air.

Pulp A wet mass.

Recycle To use something, such as a material, again.

Reflects When something, such as light, bounces back from a surface.

Sieves Strainers.

Starch A substance found in plants that is used for stiffening.

Further information

Books

Environment Detective Investigates: Reducing & Recycling Waste
Jen Green, Wayland 2010

Paper (Recycling and Reusing Materials), Ruth Thomson and Neil Thomson,
Franklin Watts, 2006

Trash and Recycling: Paper Making Kid Kit, Stephanie Turnbull, Usborne Books, 2007

Websites

www.recyclenow.com
Lots of information on recycling with fact files on paper recycling,
and a video to watch.

www.recyclezone.org.uk
A fun site with activities, quiz questions and lots of facts and information.

www.paper.org.uk
A website all about paper, with a section for children including a video of the paper
making process.

Note to parents and teachers: Every effort has been made by the Publishers
to ensure that the websites in this book are suitable for children, that they
are of the highest educational value, and that they contain no
inappropriate or offensive material. However, because of the nature of the
Internet, it is impossible to guarantee that the contents of these sites will not
be altered. We strongly advise that Internet access is supervised by a
responsible adult.

Index